The Promise

And when I die the birds shall sing.
They shall sing a threnody for me.
And when I die the clouds shall still part the heavens.
They shall weep rain for me.
And when I die the waves shall still form in the seas.
They shall break land with a roar for me.
And when I die the trees shall still grow.
They shall sigh in the wind for me.
And when I die my soul shall still go on.
It shall break free and find God for me.

Acknowledgements:
'The refugee' was included in the anthology 'Voices in the
Wind': International Society of Poets, edited by Joy L Esterby,
published by Jeffery Franz, 1996.

Lindsey, Patrick and Dermot O'Neill would like to thank Liam
and Alison Fahy, Phil Maxey, Leni Dipple and Lee Smith for
their help and encouragement with this project and all friends
and family for their support.

Contents

The Promise

Foreword

Foreword

This is a selection of poetry written by my mother, Celia O'Neill. Mum began writing at an early age and her talent was recognised whilst at school where she won a nationwide competition. She excelled at English Literature during A-levels and went on to study History and French at the University of East Anglia. Mum had various professional roles during her working life – ranging from Librarian and Archivist, to Executive Recruiter – but it was through writing that she really found her passion. On most mornings she would be up at the break of dawn to work on her novels and many times I would come down for breakfast to find the dining room table commandeered. It was a sight for bleary eyes to behold: folders of manuscript, covered from top to bottom in near illegible script, a seated figure hunched to a crescent and a scrawling hand ablaze, feverishly propelled by a mind not content to respect the rules of the ungodly hour in which it worked.

It was this passion and level of commitment that saw Mum win prizes in international competitions for her poems, some of which were included in published anthologies, but there was no collection published that consisted solely of her own poems. *The Poet's Eye* is a collection of her poems that were bought together posthumously. The poems here lie broadly in two main kinds with various other topics and themes woven in. The first kind considers (what Mum liked to discuss with us until well into many a night) the more poignant side of personal experience we, or others, may face; love, family, spirituality, loss, choice, ageing, death and God. The second kind details the smaller 'first world problems' (and perks!) that come and go but yet remain integral to our lives. To talk with

Mum, one would often be engaged in a topic at either end of this spectrum and I think the poems here perfectly express that duality of her persona.

Mum was, by her own admission, a bit of an 'outsider', never content to do things (or think!) much like everyone else, and this in turn cultivated her particular way of embracing her own experiences and those of others with whom she felt an affinity. She was deeply empathetic to the tragedies which people face, as expressed in poems such as 'The refugee' and 'To a spouse with Alzheimers'. She was in awe of the metaphysical nature of ourselves and of situations: 'The people I never knew', 'If Nana had married Arthur Underwood'; and she wasn't afraid to embrace the darker, more macabre side of herself in poems such as 'The stalker' and 'Crows at high tide'. Mum was never shy and was always only a step away from poking fun at herself, as shown in 'Relaxation tape' and 'Yoga'.

Although melancholy manifests in some of Mum's poems, there is always evidence of an undeniable omnipresent spirit; from the stories she created and illustrated as a child, the small 'Post-it' note messages she'd leave for me if she were out, to her novels and the poems collected here, all contain the endearingly playful idiosyncrasies that made her unique and that we loved her for.

Patrick O'Neill

* * * * *

You see merely an old grey stone, whereas I see still life magic.

Celia O'Neill

The poet's eye

I do not regard things in the way you do,
I take a very different sort of view.
I note all the little oddities that pass you by,
For I look at my surroundings with the poet's eye.

You see merely an old grey stone,
  whereas I see still-life magic,
You observe only what's on the surface,
  and I think that's tragic.
You let your mind simply wander
  instead of allowing it to fly,
When the Child is father of the Man
  you'll see with the poet's eye.

The people I never knew

I find I just can't forget
The people I never met.
Faces I can never know,
But oh how you haunt me so!
Why does a higher Providence decree
That some encounters are never to be?
Kindred spirits who can take no pleasure
In what they know not and cannot measure.
When my life is nearly through,
And its well-known pleasures but fleeting and few,
I'll think about the people I never knew,
Was that perhaps me and you?

Dolly Pentreath (d. 1777)

I saw the plaque outside the house,
Near picturesque Mousehole harbour,
Which commemorated her name
As the last native Cornish speaker.
I gazed on the simple pink-washed stone walls
That saw therein the extinction
Not just of one unknown individual,
But that of an entire language itself.

Hunstanton Promenade, 1970

Huddled in a corner shop in winter,
Watching the iron-grey seas
Whipped up by soughing winds
And lashed by driving rain;
A scenario to depress the stoutest of hearts.
But hand in hand over cold tea and curling sandwiches,
We are warm with the knowledge of our new-found love.

The quiet man

No, you never set the world on fire,
You just made it a better place to be,
With your quiet wisdom and gentle ways
You showed the more important things to me.

So you didn't have a lot to say,
But you had a lot of love to give,
With your pleasure in the little things,
You showed me a different way to live.

For the quietest presence will speak the loudest
Only when it is to be encountered no more,
And then at last we can fully appreciate
What we may well have taken for granted before?

(I know) I'm losing you

Let me down gently when you choose to break my heart,
Not with harsh words, looks and scowls,
But with little kindnesses and smiles.
Don't let me see you turn away from me abruptly forever,
Rather do it softly, slowly,
As the soul leaves the body of an aged person,
Each day bringing
a fresh loosening of the will to hold on to life.
That way I can surely grow resigned
to what I know is inevitable,
And accept the death of my own heart's life
with a suitable equanimity.

Transience

I wrote a message to you my love, in the sand,
Obliterated by the sea's encroaching hand,
Like the tears that will gradually wash away
The heartache you inflicted on me yesterday.
If tears meant pearls then I'd be rich for evermore,
But they'll dry just as surely as stones on the shore,
As castles in the air, proved all my hopes and dreams,
Slipping through my fingers like those soft sandy streams.
Nothing remains of the imprints my fingers made
As nothing will remain of the love I once gave …

For those in peril…

We were ships that passed in the night.
But for one brief shining moment
Our vessels found safe harbour,
Only to hit the rocks once more.

The stalker

I think about you both night and day,
I just cannot shake your face away,
It is etched before me as if in stone,
I am like a dog obsessed with a bone.
I am there whatever you may do,
With you, whoever else is there too.
The silent spectre as others feast on,
I am still there long after they are gone,
Impotent to leave, impotent to fulfil
A love that you never quite managed to kill …
A love that can yet survive on nothing at all:
It's your memory alone that keeps me in thrall.
Although we have been many years apart,
Darling, I stalk you daily in my heart.

Barriers

Brick walls and glass ceilings,
Finite universes and undeclared feelings,
The invisible chains that bind us to the lives we chose before
Our hearts knew their own minds at last.
Is it too late to reopen the door?

Shedding skins

As the snake sloughs off his outer layer,
So too do I with my redundant thoughts and dreams.
One has many reincarnations in just one lifetime
Or perhaps that's just the way it seems?
Life's a learning curve, and the aims that go with it
Must be discarded sometimes like a dried-up husk,
From larva to chrysalis and then to butterfly,
One glorious shining moment of self-revelation
Before we finally bite the dust?

Buried at sea

You belong to the elements now,
A free spirit in death
Just as you were in life.
No box could be enough to contain
Your irrepressible zest for the universe.
You shall ride the waves untrammelled,
For as long as this earth still turns on its axis,
With seagulls and ships for company,
Alone but never lonely,
While the sun shines on you by day
And the moon and stars steer your passage at night.
And every time I come down to the water's edge
I know you will be there,
And that one day I too will join you.

The wrong generation

Oh beautiful young man that I see before me in the street,
In another far-distant time, why oh why did we not meet?
I should have known you then, long ago
Before my face and hands wrinkled so,
How eloquently these now dull and rheumy eyes
Would have spoken to your answering orbs
In which sweet love would have been awoken!
I see those eyes light up now for a girl, pretty as I used to be,
If time hadn't been so cruel to us both
That girl would have been me!
Why, sixty years ago I would have put her in the shade,
Before the years took their toll and my looks began to fade.
But aged and infirm now I can only stop and bewail
The still-young heart inside me that must beat fast to no avail.

Grown old

Your face is lined and your hair has gone grey,
So is mine for we have both had our day.
Once you were strong and your body lean and lithe,
Loving you made me feel good to be alive.
Time is slow but inexorable and the years gently roll,
Our hearts stay obscenely young,
it's our bodies that take the toll.
I look at you now and see what I once knew before,
Why must I want that which I can surely have no more?

To a spouse with Alzheimer's

I know you but tragically you no longer know me,
You see me but you do not recognise what you see.
I am a stranger whom you once loved but now no longer know,
You follow me around aimlessly where'er I choose to go.
You obey me with the blind confidence
you must have displayed as a child,
But without that accompanying spark of spirit
that doubtless beguiled.
In this paradoxical illness you are both alive and dead,
How can I see in this mute zombie the person I once did wed?
Briefly, so tantalisingly,
you have had your moments of lucidity,
When you returned to being you,
only to return to this stupidity.
Perhaps it is as well for both of us
that these frustrating moments are no more,
And I can define clearer the two yous:
this shell and the lover I once knew before.

If Nanna had married Arthur Underwood

I can't help wondering though it can do no good,
What if Nanna had married Arthur Underwood:
That ardent young suitor from her dim distant past?
A seven-year courtship that was doomed not to last ...
But if it had – no Grandpa would have come into her life
To sweep her off her feet and make her his beloved wife.
So, where would I and my poor dear mother have been,
Just lost in the universe, unknown and unseen?
All our hopes and dreams, sadly never to be known,
Our potential snuffed out in the nothingness zone ...
But it doesn't apply, for the thing ended as it should,
And Nanna married Grandpa, and <u>not</u> Arthur Underwood!
(Who trundled off someplace to nurse a broken heart –
Not very lucky in love was our good friend Art!)
And so the great day of my birth eventually dawned,
But not the lost generation that just might have been spawned
If things had happened in the way that they just could
And Nanna had married poor Arthur Underwood.

The Aborted Child

Every time your 'should-have-been' birthday
Comes around I ask myself why,
I decided to play God and deemed
That you should not live but must die.

If I could but have my time again,
I'd treasure that missing part
Of my soul that I shall never know:
The blueprint who breaks my heart.

You must be one of the angels now,
Poor boy/girl child manqué of mine,
Look down from Heaven and pity me if you can,
For to err is human but to forgive, divine.

Still-birth

Ten tiny pink toes and ten tiny fingers,
The memory of my child still lingers,
God made her so perfect and in every way whole,
Except that He took away her immortal soul …

The Adopted Child

You are my beloved child but not child of my love,
Gift of another woman and not from Him above,
I shall love you the more because I know you are not mine,
For that lost blueprint of myself I shall no longer pine.
I'll not wonder at the little things that show you as my clone,
As your growing mind and body start to echo my own,
Rather I must mould you to myself and the best of my ways,
By dint of my own efforts throughout the oncoming days.

Abandoned dog in a car

He waits, St Sebastian's canine relation,
Martyrdom not through arrows but a goldfish bowl on wheels,
Perfectly quiet, with such sad resignation,
As the noonday sun high in the sky remorselessly steals.

Chocolate-coloured eyes gaze up at me in mute appeal,
How eloquently they speak through the scorching glass!
I shake my head at the impotent anger that I feel,
How many more minutes of this torment must pass?

The sun drops ever lower down, and by and by,
His owner returns to find the dog lying there prone,
Sentenced by his unthinking carelessness to die,
He'd brought his best friend back a nice big fat juicy bone …

The refugee

I live among those neither hostile nor friendly,
Far from my homeland, fated never to return.
The memories that will have to last me a lifetime
Are a few scattered trinkets I had with me then.
At first, all freely gave of their sympathy
To one whose problem was not their concern.
Such surface pity could only be temporary,
As commiseration gave way to complacency.
Life had to go on, and their minds were turned
To thoughts more comfortable and familiar.
I was tolerated; my worries too became nebulous
To those unable to comprehend a tragedy
Which they had not personally experienced.
Ah, if I too could conveniently forget as they,
But my grief does not stop for me,
It continues irrevocably.

Daleks

They glide on invisible castors like crinoline ladies,
With antennae like pincers, these ministers from Hades.
Their death rays are pointed and flight is too late,
As I cower behind the sofa, I hear: 'Ex-ter-min-ate!'

Opera

I've cried watching Cav and Pag,
And bawled over Butterfly,
Turandot reduced me to tears,
Why does everyone have to die?

I've groaned for poor old Gilda
And wept buckets at Bohème.
One thing I know, wherever I go
The story is pretty much the same.

La Traviata and Tosca simply tear me apart
And Lohengrin leaves me lachrymose,
When it comes to being happy and gay, no way José,
In opera that's how the story goes.

I've sighed with Salome and Sieglinde,
You know there's really just no reason or rhyme
Why the composers all seem to decree
That everyone must have such a rotten time!

Crows at high tide

I watch them fly squawking up the beach,
Snapping at seagulls in their flapping ebony cloaks,
As they soar umbrella-like on to my roof,
Huddling together like a coven of witches,
Or a scene from a Hitchcock film ...
They regard me with vague malevolent uninterest.
As I slowly back away indoors,
I imagine their obscene midnight faces
Pressed hard against shattering glass,
Blood-spattered beaks penetrating, raking
At living, tortured flesh ...
Shuddering, I turn aside and close the curtains,
With a comforting click I switch on the TV,
And there they all are on the screen ...

Yoga

I've tried the Lion Pose
And I've tackled the Plough,
I've done a Head-Lotus
And kept upright somehow.

I've checked on my chakras
And aw-uh-mmmed with the best,
I've done twists, clasps and rolls
And expanded my chest.

I've done squats, bows and head stands
And performed a complete breath,
And after all these push-ups
I'm simply feeling like death.

I've done all the postures
But alas and alack,
All I've in fact managed
Is to do in my back!

Making waves at the pool

Why is it that it seems to be
Schools all choose the same time as me?
Why does the cubicle I select
Have to be so exceedingly wet?
Why does the locker that I pick
Have the one key that doesn't fit?
Why must the coin that I am then required to feed
Be the one I don't possess – but the one I shall need?
Why (when I get it!) must it always be my luck
That it's <u>my</u> locker money that has to get stuck?
Why is it that when I'm ready (at last!) for my swim,
A keep-fit class is using half of it as a gym?
Why is it someone always has to dive
Into the very spot where I arrive?
Why is it I always seem to cop
The tidal wave from a belly-flop?
Why is it when I choose an empty lane
Everyone has to follow? It's insane!
Why is it that the showers are always full
The minute I get myself out of the pool?
Why (when I get one) do I always have to find
The water's freezing or boiling? It's such a bind!
Why is it that the hairdryer doesn't work
And I'm left sopping wet, looking a right berk!
Why is it I remember only when I am out of the gate
I forgot to collect my locker money and now it's too late…?
Why is it when I know it's such a blinking bore,
I'll still find myself coming back next week for more?!

Relaxation tape

One sound of that sweet siren voice,
With its well-modulated rise and flow,
Both comforting and authoritative,
And I am letting go, letting go …

Grip your hands together tightly and relax,
Breath in and out and keep it nice and slow,
Make your biceps and your triceps muscles contract,
Then release them soft and gently and let go …

Screw your face up, purse your lips together firmly,
Damn! The phone's ringing, oh hang on a mo',
I've got to smooth out the creases in my forehead,
And make sure I'm keeping limp and letting go …

They've rung off and the voice drones on hypnotically,
And I'm afraid I'm feeling rather a Sleepy Joe,
I doze through the rest of the instructions,
And find that I've been too literally 'letting go …'

Achilles' heel

I took advice from so-called experts
And correctly aligned all the doors,
I painted my walls soothing colours,
Stuck the right kinds of rugs on the floors.
I let tinkling wind-chimes swing gently in the hall,
Put Chinese Fu dogs to guard the exterior,
Made absolutely sure that the bed faced due south,
And fresh-cut flowers bedecked the interior.
A clock with three hands adorned the mantel,
My sofas were arranged to form a square,
Candles burned brightly to cleanse the auras,
I hung up lots of pictures everywhere.
Books to stimulate and bring wisdom sat on my shelves,
From the ceiling I hung up a crystal chandelier,
Cushions were scattered to encourage relaxation,
No chance for evil spirits to find a way in here!
Good fortune would surely smile on me now,
But there was one thing that I failed to do,
Yes, I protected my abode with Feng Shui,
But left my heart unprotected against you …

Paradise Lost (The new housing estate)

Sheep may no longer safely graze
In fields and across bridle-ways,
The grass has gone from beneath their feet,
Drowned in a hard sea of concrete.
Inviting vistas are now just a distant dream,
Des reses have replaced the scene,
Nice views and homes – you can't have both –
Not in an area of designated growth!

Rural suburbia

Foxes scavenge among bins,
Bats hang upside down in lofts,
Runner beans and raspberries grow on the cane,
As the smoke from the factory chimney wafts.
The small token patch of greensward
Sits right in the middle of the estate,
Is it the country or is it the town?
To be both and neither, our fate.

Thoroughly Modern Menace

What a right pain it is, begging your pardon,
This dark oppressive scourge of the back garden.
An ugly all-pervasive would-be creature of the night,
Wherever it spreads itself it just blocks out all the light.
Shooting its coarse tentacles to the skies without fail,
Leaving wrecked neighbourly relationships in its trail.
Robbing the soil of nutrients and fertility,
One way or another it's one great liability!
Hell on Earth for gardeners comes in many many guises:
Like an obscene green tidal wave the foliage just rises –
Twenty foot, thirty foot, now forty foot or more,
If this growth continues there'll soon be outright war …
Everything in the garden's no longer fine and dandy,
When Him Next Door has put in some fast-growing leylandii!

The colour of the wind

Is it the mottled white and brown of the heifers –
Stringy tails twitched by the gentlest of zephyrs?
Is it the soft autumnal golden tint of the leaves
As it playfully swirls them up high as it doth please?
Is it the mauve of berries scattered from the vine
On which the hungry birds will soon gratefully dine?
Is it the many-hued green of deciduous trees
That shiver and shake in the ever-freshening breeze?
Is it the myriad shades of my attire –
Spinning just like tops from the rotary dryer?
Is it the raw frozen blue of my beleaguered face
As it wraps me around hard in its wintry embrace?
Is it the wild bible-black night of the storm
That howls around the house where I'm snug in the warm?
Is it the glass-grey of the sea as the waves rescind,
For who can possibly know the colour of the wind?

Time management

What do we do with all the extra time that we save
When we pop ready-meals into the microwave?
How do we use the hours that we must therefore accrue
When we drive to the station, shops, schools and workplace
too?
All those precious nano-seconds and minutes
that we've fought so hard to earn,
Why, we'll spend attending new-age courses
exhorting us folk how to learn
To do all the things that we are surely doing already today:
Saving oodles of time in order just to fritter it all away …

Lies

You can tell untruths with every part of your body,
The lips that smile as they smoothly speak their falsehoods,
The head that alternately nods and shakes,
The hands that gesticulate,
And the feet that tap their mendacious emphasis.
But the windows of the soul, like your sins,
Will always find you out.

A Scottish scene

The great shepherd silently watches over his flock
As they pass bleating across the cool waters below,
Through scree and boulders and gleaming, rain-washed stones
And on to the soft, springy heather they go.
A solitary wildcat presses back tufted ears
And pads swiftly along with feet that are sure,
A mountain goat feasts on the bright yellow gorse
Under the watchful shadow of Buchaille Etive Mor.

Cuarenta y Tres

I came across it six months later,
One gloomy winter's day,
A miniature bottle lying forgotten,
In the far depths of a kitchen cupboard.
But one sip of that smooth honey-sweet nectar
Transports me back to the warmth of a summer's day,
With bright skies and dusty pavements,
Cicadas and olive groves
And holiday friendships that never mature,
When I first tasted that rich ambrosia
From a rough-hewn cask
In the cool interior
Of a Spanish bodega.

Italy

Parmesan and pasta,
La Gioconda and gelati,
Bottom-pinching and 'Buon giornos',
Frescoes and Frascati.

La Bohème and la Scala,
Gina Lollobrigida and Gerona,
Antipasti and 'Arrivedercis',
Volcanos and Verona.

Sun-dried tomatoes and tutti-frutti,
Catacombs and Caravaggio,
Pisa and 'per favores',
Via Appia and Viareggio.

'Molto bellissimas',
Culture and Chianti,
I once spent a holiday
In Sestri Levante.

Sunshine and Siena,
'Parliamo Italiano?'
Let's go visit the Uffizi,
It's just across the Arno.

Stonehenge

Modern-day pagans and new-age travellers
Gaze longingly at their fenced-off spiritual home,
And dream of solstices and azimuths,
Heel stones and slaughter stones,
Where they once tried to re-create
A lost spiritual dawn of Druidism
Where their supposed ancestors waved sprigs of mistletoe,
Played ip dip with friend or foe,
And made unspeakable sacrifices
In wicker baskets of their fellow folk,
In order to appease the Spirit of the Oak.

Heads (not talking)

I saw them once on a documentary,
Great, gaunt forbidding pieces of stone,
Their countenances rough-hewn and unyielding,
Some pointing to the sky, some fallen in the grass,
But all possessed of a strange and savage dignity.
They bear their silent testimony to a time long-vanished,
Which we cannot hope to ever fully comprehend.
Over remote and barren wind-swept hillsides,
The mysterious watchers of Easter Island
Keep their long and ceaseless vigil.

Cro-Magnon Man at Lascoux

The bold and graceful lines of your paintings
Bear their own spare but eloquent testimony
To your undoubted sophistication.
Oh you who lived and hunted
Full twelve thousand years ago,
Tall, straight and God-like,
Alongside primitive Neanderthal,
Were you not indeed the heirs of lost Atlantis itself?

Mummies in the Vatican Museum

Of all the treasures that I saw:
Gold and silver, precious stones,
Rich and rare antiquities galore,
I was moved to wonder most at fragile old bones,
For the things that will always stay with me,
In my mind's eye never to be forgot,
Are those black leathery scraps of humanity,
That thousands of years were unable to rot.

If there were no God

If there were truly no God,
Nobody to see the way
That I do things in my life,
Would I still freely decide
By his own rules to abide,
As I do usually today?

If there were without a doubt no God,
How much finer then would it make me
In all my altruistic moments,
Knowing there would be no reckoning,
No potential hell-fires beckoning,
And still a selfless person be?

All worshipping the same God?

My God is on my side
And your God is apparently on yours.
My God looks after me,
While yours espouses a different cause.
If we both get to Heaven,
Which one of 'em will we see?
If they're the same God after all,
Will He side with you or with me?

Reincarnation

Is there a sense of déjà vu,
In everything we see and do?
Have we really been here before,
Are we coming back for more?!
The notion is mad!
Who could possibly wish to die,
In order to come back as a beetle or a fly?
I'm honestly not sure I can stay the distance,
If I have to cope with more than one existence.

Once is quite enough you know,
I'll settle for hell-fire if I must,
But when I finally leave this earth,
I want the dust to stay as dust!

The solitary worshipper

Lay aside your cares as you enter within,
For they surely have no place here.
Walk forward slowly, with measured steps,
Kneel quietly amidst the silence,
Breathe deep the peace of ages,
Bow your head discreetly and reverently,
And open up your soul to the Lord;
For there is no better place to be alone
Than the place where one is never truly alone.

The things I never did

I never climbed up the Himalayas,
Sailed on a felucca down the Nile,
Took the scariest ride at Chessington,
Divorced seven husbands Hollywood-style,
I never got up early to embrace the dawn,
Recited 'Eskimo Nell' at a posh works do,
But the thing that I regret the most
Was that I never said: 'I love you.'
I never learnt Sanskrit, Flemish or Serbo-Croat,
Tap-dancing, how to trainspot and do the fandango,
I never quite mastered the art of macramé,
Or managed to eat without mess a fresh mango,
I never got beyond Grade 1 at the piano,
Rode a camel all the way south down to Timbuktu,
But the thing that I regret the most
Was that I never said: 'I love you.'
I never quite got the hand of public speaking,
Remembered to say: 'Lay on, Macduff',
Watched 'Your Life in their Hands' without getting squeamish,
Dared to sunbathe and swim in the buff,
I never ate fish and chips straight from a newspaper,
Quite managed to see the other fellow's point of view,
But the thing that I regret the most
Was that I never said: 'I love you.'
I never plucked up enough courage to deal with spiders,
Got a fabulous bargain on the first day of a sale,
Acquired a tan without resembling a lobster,
Looked interesting when my poor skin appeared pale,
I never stood on a soap box in Hyde Park Corner,
Made a chain from daisies in the early-morning dew,
But the thing that I regret the most
Was that I never said: 'I love you.'

I never led a horse from the winners' enclosure,
Finished off 'The Times' crossword without cheating,
I never hung upside-down to kiss the Blarney Stone,
Enjoyed a love that was more than just fleeting,
I never got a man to drink champagne from my slipper,
Served at a posh dinner party – a plate of Irish stew,
But the thing that I regret the most
Was that I never said: 'I love you.'
I never got to dive straight in at the deep end,
Played hopscotch with the kids without feeling a fool,
I never spent a night at the Savoy for the hell of it,
Knew the proper way to deal with a great big plate of moules,
I never quite worked out how to use the possessive pronoun,
So much unsaid and undone that I must surely always rue,
I never got roaring drunk, only maudlin,
And I left it too late to say: 'I love you...'

Prayer for a Good Death

When I pass over to the other side,
  please let it be from here:
This very special place on God's earth
  which to me has been most dear.
What more congenial way
  to begin that last journey into the unknown
Than from the familiar surroundings
  of my own dear sweet beloved home?
With kindly well-loved faces
  to speed me gently on my way,
And wish the traveller luck
  on this most strange and poignant day.
Like a Pharoh surrounded by his trappings
  to meet that final goal,
I'll face with equanimity
  the passage of my immortal soul.

The day after you died

The sun blazes effulgently
  and birds in trees abide,
How dare life go on in this way
  just after you have died?
How come these birds are warbling
  a series of notes so gay?
For shame! They ought to hide
  their brash uncaring selves away.
Does the whole cosmos have no heart at all
  permitting a sky so blue?
It should be dark and grey like lead
  out of respect for my dearest you.
And the flowers opening their petals
  in this most unseemly way,
Why aren't they drooping their heads right down
  on this highly sorrowful day?
Were you <u>not</u> master of your universe,
  set above all other things?
But cruel Death lays his icy hand
  not just on commoners but kings.
Be we higher than the beasts,
  we are levelled by the same natural law
That says that life must go on regardless,
  exactly the same as before.

Lightning Source UK Ltd.
Milton Keynes UK
UKOW04f1131141017
310965UK00001B/39/P